THE SIMPLICITY WITH GROUNDED WISDOM

EMBRACING AUTHENTICITY IN A COMPLEX WORLD

DR. MINAKSHI BANSAL

Made with ♥ on the Notion Press Platform
www.notionpress.com

DEDICATION

To all those who dare to live a life that is true to their own hearts, who embrace their unique gifts and imperfections, and who strive to make a positive difference in the world.

♡♡♡

Contents

Contents

Contents

Prayer

"Om Poornamadah Poornamidam Poornaat Poornamudachyate, Poornasya Poornamaadaya Poornamevavashishyate"

"Om Shantih, Shantih, Shantih"

The literal interpretation of this mantra is: That which is Absolute, This which is Absolute, Absolute arises from Absolute, If Absolute is removed from Absolute, Absolute remains

This mantra is a reminder of the fundamental truth that all of existence is rooted in the Absolute. It is a reminder that the Absolute is the source of all that is, and that it is ever-present, even when all else is taken away. It is a reminder of the peace that comes from understanding and accepting this truth.

Om Peace, Peace, Peace.

About The Author

Dr. Minakshi Bansal, born in the bustling metropolis of Delhi, India, has led a life steeped in artistry, scholarly pursuit, and an unwavering commitment to societal betterment. Following her marriage, she relocated to Ahmedabad, Gujarat, where she has since blossomed into a multifaceted beacon of inspiration for many. Dr. Minakshi is not only recognized as a gifted artist in the realm of Fine Arts but also as an esteemed author, a devoted social worker and a dedicated research scholar in Psychology. Her journey, marked by a profound dedication to elevating those around her, especially the downtrodden and underprivileged children of society, is a testament to her deep-seated belief in the transformative power of engagement and empathy.

From her earliest days, Minakshi was distinguished by an insatiable appetite for reading. Her literary universe was inhabited by characters and narratives that spanned ethical tales, motivational and inspirational stories, and the mythic parables imbued with life lessons. This voracious reading habit was not merely for personal edification but was driven by a desire to distill and disseminate the essence of these narratives to foster the development of students and peers alike. She was particularly captivated by the lives and teachings of historical figures and spiritual leaders such as Adi Shankaracharya, Swami Vivekananda, Dr. APJ Abdul Kalam, Mahamana Pandit Madan Mohan Malviya, Mahatma Gandhi, Sardar Vallabhai Patel, and Vinoba Bhave, among others. Their philosophies and life stories fueled her ambition to embody their ideals of resilience, selflessness, and relentless pursuit of knowledge.

Dr. Minakshi's academic and practical engagement with psychology has been equally noteworthy. As a research scholar, her focus has been on exploring the intricate tapestry of the human psyche, aiming to unlock the potential for psychological well-being and societal harmony. Her scholarly work is complemented by her active involvement in social work, where she employs her academic insights to make tangible differences in the lives of the underprivileged. Her endeavours in social work are characterized by an innovative approach that combines traditional wisdom with contemporary psychological practices to address the multifaceted challenges faced by these communities.

Her artistic talents, another facet of her diverse capabilities, are not merely a personal passion but also serve as a medium through which she communicates and connects with others. Her art, rich in symbolism and emotional depth, reflects her philosophical inquiries and social concerns, offering viewers a glimpse into the breadth of her intellect and the depth of her compassion.

In addition to her contributions to the arts and social sciences, Dr. Minakshi has embraced the healing arts of Pranic Healing, mastering the techniques developed by Master Choa Kok Sui. This practice, which focuses on the manipulation of Prana or life energy to heal the body and aura, has been both a personal journey of discovery and a means through which she extends her healing touch to others. Her proficiency in Pranic Healing is complemented by her advocacy and teaching of various forms of meditation aimed at rejuvenation, personal betterment, and the cultivation of harmony within individuals and communities alike.

Dr. Minakshi's life is a narrative of relentless pursuit, not just of personal achievement but of the upliftment and empowerment of society at large. Her diverse interests and talents—spanning the arts, literature, psychology, and the healing practices—converge on a singular path of service. She embodies the spirit of the luminaries who inspired her, channelling their legacy through her actions and teachings. Through her books, art, and social initiatives, she continues to inspire a new generation to embark on their own journeys of self-discovery, resilience, and altruism.

Her commitment to social betterment, particularly her focus on uplifting underprivileged children, reflects a deep understanding of the transformative potential of education and personal development. By integrating her knowledge of psychology, her artistic sensibilities, and her healing practices, Dr. Bansal has developed a holistic approach to social work that addresses both the immediate needs and the long-term well-being of the communities she serves.

As an author, Dr. Minakshi's writings offer a blend of inspirational insights, practical wisdom, and reflective contemplations drawn from her extensive reading and life experiences. Her books serve as a guide for those seeking to navigate the complexities of life with grace, resilience, and purpose. Through her narratives, she extends an invitation to her readers to explore the depths of their own potential and to contribute meaningfully to the collective well-being of society.

In Dr. Minakshi Bansal, we find a remarkable synthesis of the artist, the scholar, the healer, and the social activist. Her life's work stands as a beacon of hope and a source of inspiration for individuals seeking to make a difference in the world. Her story is a compelling reminder of the power of individual action, rooted in compassion and driven by a profound commitment to the betterment of humanity. Dr. Minakshi's legacy is not just in the tangible outcomes of her efforts but in the enduring spirit of inquiry, empathy, and service that she embodies.

Preface

In the tapestry of life, there are moments when the clamor of the world fades, and a gentle whisper emerges from within, guiding us toward a path of greater clarity, peace, and fulfillment. This book is an invitation to heed that whisper, to embrace the profound simplicity that lies at the heart of wisdom and authenticity.

My journey toward this understanding has been a winding one, filled with both triumphs and setbacks. I have navigated the complexities of modern life, striving for success, recognition, and material possessions. Yet, amidst the external achievements, I often felt a nagging sense of emptiness, a longing for something more meaningful and enduring.

It was through a series of personal challenges and transformative experiences that I began to glimpse the power of simplicity. I discovered that true happiness and fulfillment are not found in the accumulation of things, but in the quality of our relationships, the depth of our experiences, and the alignment of our actions with our values.

I learned that wisdom is not about knowing all the answers, but about embracing the unknown with humility and curiosity. It's about learning from our mistakes, seeking guidance from those who have walked before us, and trusting our intuition. Wisdom is a lifelong journey of self-discovery, of uncovering the timeless truths that reside within us all.

Authenticity, I realized, is the courage to be ourselves, to embrace our unique gifts and imperfections. It's about letting go of the need to please others or conform to societal expectations, and instead, choosing to live a life that is true to our own hearts. Authenticity is a beacon of light, illuminating our path and guiding us towards a life of greater joy, purpose, and fulfillment.

In the pages of this book, I share my personal experiences, insights, and reflections on the journey towards simplicity, wisdom, and authenticity. I offer practical guidance and tools for cultivating these qualities in your own life, from decluttering your home and simplifying your schedule to cultivating mindfulness, embracing your intuition, and setting healthy boundaries.

I believe that by embracing simplicity, wisdom, and authenticity, we can create a life that is both meaningful and fulfilling. We can find peace in the present moment, cultivate deeper connections with ourselves and others, and make a positive impact on the world around us.

This book is not a prescription for a perfect life; there is no such thing. It's an invitation to embark on a journey of self-discovery, to explore the depths of your own being, and to uncover the wisdom that resides within you. It's a call to live a life that is true to your own heart, a life that is both simple and profound.

I invite you to join me on this journey. Let us together explore the transformative power of simplicity, wisdom, and authenticity. Let us embrace the challenges and uncertainties of life with courage and grace. And let us create a world that is more compassionate, just, and sustainable for ourselves and for generations to come.

The journey begins now.

Dr. Minakshi Bansal
Social Activist
Ahmedabad, Gujarat, Bharat

ONE

The Call of Simplicity: Rediscovering the Allure of a Less Cluttered Life

In a world overflowing with information, possessions, and endless options, the call of simplicity beckons like a gentle whisper, promising a path to tranquility and contentment. It's a call that resonates deeply within us, urging us to step back from the chaos and rediscover the allure of a less cluttered life.

We live in an era of abundance, where consumerism reigns supreme and the pursuit of more is often equated with success. But amidst the constant bombardment of advertisements, social media updates, and the relentless pressure to keep up with the Joneses, many of us find ourselves yearning for something more meaningful, something that goes beyond the accumulation of material possessions.

The call of simplicity is a recognition that true wealth lies not in the abundance of things, but in the quality of our experiences, relationships, and inner peace. It's an invitation to shed the unnecessary burdens that weigh us down and embrace a life that is lighter, more intentional, and ultimately more fulfilling.

The allure of a less cluttered life lies in its ability to free us from the distractions and anxieties that often accompany a life of excess. When we simplify our lives, we create space for what truly matters. We have more time to devote to our passions, to nurture our relationships, and to simply be present in the moment.

Embracing simplicity is not about deprivation or asceticism; it's about making conscious choices and prioritizing what brings us joy and meaning. It's about letting go of the things that no longer serve us, whether it's material possessions, commitments, or even negative thought patterns.

The journey towards a less cluttered life begins with decluttering our physical surroundings. This can be as simple as clearing out a closet, donating unused items, or organizing our homes and workspaces. As we create a more orderly and serene environment, we often find that our minds become calmer and more focused.

But decluttering goes beyond our physical possessions. It also involves simplifying our schedules, commitments, and even our digital lives. We can learn to say no to requests that don't align with our priorities, unsubscribe from email lists that overwhelm our inboxes, and limit our time on social media. By creating boundaries and setting limits, we reclaim our time and energy for what truly matters.

Simplifying our lives also involves cultivating a mindset of contentment and gratitude. When we learn to appreciate what we have, rather than constantly striving for more, we open ourselves up to a deeper sense of satisfaction and well-being. We begin to see the abundance that already exists in our lives, rather than focusing on what we lack.

Embracing simplicity doesn't mean giving up all our possessions or living a minimalist lifestyle. It's about finding a balance that works for us, one that allows us to live a life that is both fulfilling and unburdened.

In a world that often values complexity and busyness, the call of simplicity is a radical act of self-care. It's a choice to step off the treadmill of constant striving and embrace a life that is more aligned with our values and priorities. As we simplify our lives, we create space for greater joy, peace, and authenticity.

Rediscovering the allure of a less cluttered life is not a one-time event, but an ongoing process. It requires constant vigilance and a willingness to let go of what no longer serves us. But the rewards are immeasurable. When we embrace simplicity, we open ourselves up to a life that is richer, more meaningful, and ultimately more fulfilling.

Simplicity isn't about deprivation, but liberation. By shedding the excess, we create space for what truly nourishes our souls. It's a journey of discovering that less is often more.

TWO

THE ART OF SUBTRACTION: DECLUTTERING YOUR POSSESSIONS, SCHEDULE, AND MIND

In a world that constantly bombards us with messages of "more is better," the art of subtraction offers a refreshing counterpoint. It's a philosophy that encourages us to declutter our lives – not just our physical possessions, but also our schedules and minds – in order to create space for what truly matters.

Decluttering our possessions is often the first step on this journey. We live in an age of unprecedented consumerism, where acquiring new things is often seen as a path to happiness. However, the accumulation of material possessions can quickly become a burden, weighing us down with clutter and creating a sense of overwhelm.

By consciously choosing to let go of the things we no longer need or use, we can free ourselves from the tyranny of stuff. This process can be both liberating and empowering. As we sort through our belongings, we are forced to confront our attachment to material possessions and to question the value they truly hold in our lives. The act of donating, selling, or discarding unused items can be a cathartic experience, allowing us to release emotional baggage and create a sense of spaciousness in our homes.

But decluttering goes beyond our physical possessions. It also involves simplifying our schedules and commitments. In a society that glorifies busyness, it's easy to overcommit ourselves, filling our calendars with appointments, meetings, and social obligations. However, this relentless pursuit of productivity can leave us feeling exhausted, stressed, and disconnected from what truly matters.

To declutter our schedules, we must learn to prioritize and say no to requests that don't align with our values or goals. This may mean turning down invitations to events we don't genuinely want to attend, delegating tasks that can be handled by others, or simply carving out time for rest and relaxation. By creating boundaries and learning to say no, we reclaim our time and energy for the things that truly matter.

Perhaps the most challenging aspect of decluttering is addressing the clutter in our minds. Our thoughts and emotions can become as cluttered as our homes and schedules, filled with worries, anxieties, and negative self-talk. This mental clutter can cloud our judgment, hinder our creativity, and prevent us from fully experiencing the present moment.

To declutter our minds, we can turn to practices like meditation, mindfulness, and journaling. These tools can help us become more aware of our thoughts and emotions, allowing us to observe them without judgment and to let go of those that no longer serve us. By cultivating a more mindful approach to our mental landscape, we can create space for clarity, peace, and joy.

The art of subtraction is not about deprivation or minimalism for its own sake. It's about intentionally choosing what we allow into our lives, whether it's material possessions, commitments, or thoughts. By decluttering our lives, we create space for what truly matters – our relationships, our passions, our personal growth, and our well-being.

The benefits of decluttering are numerous and far-reaching. It can reduce stress and anxiety, improve focus and productivity, and foster a greater sense of contentment and gratitude. As we let go of the excess in our lives, we create space for new experiences, new relationships, and new possibilities.

Embracing the art of subtraction is an ongoing process, not a one-time event. It requires constant vigilance and a willingness to re-evaluate our choices on a regular basis. However, the rewards are well worth the effort. By simplifying our lives, we can create a life that is more intentional, more meaningful, and ultimately more fulfilling.

In the quiet moments, wisdom whispers. Listen to your intuition, that gentle nudge that guides you towards your authentic path. Trust your inner compass and embrace the unknown.

THREE

Finding Focus: Prioritizing what truly matters in a world of distractions

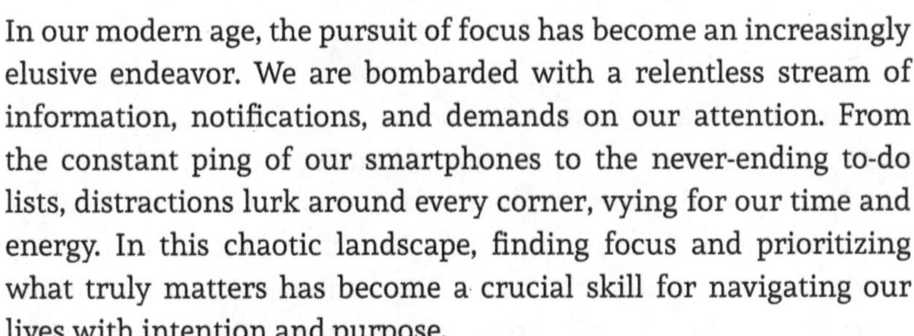

In our modern age, the pursuit of focus has become an increasingly elusive endeavor. We are bombarded with a relentless stream of information, notifications, and demands on our attention. From the constant ping of our smartphones to the never-ending to-do lists, distractions lurk around every corner, vying for our time and energy. In this chaotic landscape, finding focus and prioritizing what truly matters has become a crucial skill for navigating our lives with intention and purpose.

The ability to focus is not merely a matter of willpower or discipline; it's a conscious choice we make amidst the clamor of competing priorities. It requires us to step back from the whirlwind of daily life and take a deliberate pause to assess what truly holds significance for us.

The first step in finding focus is to identify our core values and priorities. What are the principles that guide our lives? What are the goals and aspirations that we hold most dear? By clarifying our values, we create a compass that can guide our decisions and actions, helping us to stay on course even when faced with countless distractions.

Once we have a clear understanding of our values, we can begin to prioritize our activities and commitments accordingly. This involves discerning between what is truly important and what is merely urgent or convenient. It means learning to say no to distractions and requests that don't align with our values, even when they seem tempting or harmless.

In a world that glorifies busyness and multitasking, prioritizing what truly matters often requires us to slow down and simplify our lives. This may mean decluttering our schedules, letting go of commitments that no longer serve us, and creating space for stillness and reflection. By creating a more intentional and less cluttered life, we free up our time and energy to focus on what truly matters.

Technology, while undoubtedly a powerful tool, can also be a major source of distraction. Our smartphones, with their constant notifications and endless streams of information, can easily hijack our attention and derail our focus. To reclaim our focus, we may need to set boundaries with technology, such as designating specific times for checking email and social media, or creating device-free zones in our homes.

Finding focus is not a one-time event, but an ongoing practice that requires constant vigilance and self-awareness. It's about cultivating a mindful approach to our lives, where we are fully present in each moment and attuned to our inner compass.

One powerful tool for cultivating focus is mindfulness meditation. By practicing mindfulness, we learn to observe our thoughts and emotions without judgment, allowing us to become more aware of the distractions that pull us away from our center. With regular practice, mindfulness can help us to cultivate a more focused and centered mind, even in the midst of chaos.

Another key aspect of finding focus is learning to manage our energy levels. Our ability to focus is not constant throughout the day; it ebbs and flows depending on our physical and mental state. By understanding our energy cycles, we can schedule our most important tasks for times when we are most alert and focused, and reserve less demanding tasks for times when our energy is lower.

Finding focus is not merely a matter of personal productivity; it's a way of life that can lead to greater fulfillment and well-being. When we prioritize what truly matters, we align our actions with our values, creating a sense of purpose and meaning in our lives. We become more resilient in the face of challenges, more present in our relationships, and more engaged in our work.

In a world that is constantly vying for our attention, finding focus is an act of resistance. It's a choice to reclaim our time, energy, and attention, and to direct them towards what truly matters. By cultivating focus, we not only enhance our own lives but also contribute to a more mindful and intentional world.

Authenticity is the courage to be yourself, even when the world urges you to conform. Embrace your unique quirks and imperfections, for they are the essence of your true beauty.

♡♡♡

FOUR

The Joy of Enough: Embracing Contentment and Letting Go of Excess

In our modern society, we are constantly bombarded with messages telling us that we need more – more possessions, more money, more status, more experiences. The pursuit of "more" is often seen as the key to happiness and fulfillment. However, the relentless pursuit of excess can lead to a never-ending cycle of dissatisfaction, stress, and emptiness. The "joy of enough" offers a refreshing alternative, inviting us to embrace contentment and let go of the pursuit of excess.

At its core, the joy of enough is a recognition that true happiness and fulfillment are not found in the accumulation of material possessions or external achievements. It's a shift in perspective, a realization that we already have everything we need to live a rich and meaningful life. By embracing contentment, we can break free from the insatiable desire for more and cultivate a deeper sense of gratitude and well-being.

The pursuit of excess is often fueled by a sense of lack or scarcity. We believe that if we only had more money, a bigger house, a better job, or more followers on social media, then we would finally be happy. However, this mindset is a trap, as it constantly reinforces the belief that we are not enough as we are.

The joy of enough invites us to challenge this scarcity mindset and to recognize the abundance that already exists in our lives. It encourages us to appreciate the simple pleasures, the loving relationships, the beauty of nature, and the countless blessings that surround us. By focusing on what we have, rather than what we lack, we can cultivate a sense of gratitude that can transform our lives.

Letting go of excess is not about deprivation or asceticism; it's about consciously choosing what we allow into our lives. It's about decluttering our homes, simplifying our schedules, and freeing ourselves from the weight of material possessions that no longer serve us. It's about creating space for what truly matters – our relationships, our passions, our personal growth, and our well-being.

Embracing the joy of enough also means letting go of the need for external validation. In a society that often measures our worth by our achievements and possessions, it's easy to fall into the trap of seeking approval from others. However, true contentment comes from within, from a deep sense of self-worth and self-acceptance.

The joy of enough is not a static state, but an ongoing practice. It requires us to be mindful of our thoughts and emotions, to notice when we are caught in the grip of desire or comparison, and to gently redirect our attention to the present moment. It's about cultivating a sense of inner peace and contentment that is not dependent on external circumstances.

The benefits of embracing the joy of enough are numerous and far-reaching. It can reduce stress and anxiety, improve our relationships, enhance our creativity, and foster a greater sense of purpose and meaning in our lives. By letting go of the pursuit of excess, we can free ourselves from the endless cycle of wanting and striving, and discover a deeper sense of joy and fulfillment.

In a world that constantly tells us that we need more, the joy of enough is a radical act of self-love. It's a choice to step off the treadmill of consumerism and embrace a life that is richer, more meaningful, and ultimately more fulfilling. By cultivating contentment and letting go of excess, we can discover a deeper sense of peace, joy, and gratitude that is not dependent on external circumstances.

Let go of the need for comparison, for it is a thief of joy. Celebrate your own journey, your own triumphs and struggles, and remember that everyone's path is unique.

♡♡♡

FIVE

The Slow Lane: Rediscovering the Beauty of a Slower, More Mindful Pace

In our fast-paced, hyper-connected world, the concept of slowing down can seem counterintuitive, even radical. We are constantly bombarded with messages urging us to do more, be more, and achieve more, all at breakneck speed. Yet, amidst the relentless hustle and bustle, a growing number of individuals are discovering the profound beauty and transformative power of embracing a slower, more mindful pace.

The slow lane is not about laziness or stagnation; it's a conscious choice to step off the treadmill of constant striving and embrace a more deliberate, intentional way of life. It's about savoring the present moment, appreciating the simple joys of life, and cultivating a deeper connection with ourselves, others, and the world around us.

In a society that glorifies productivity and efficiency, slowing down can feel like an act of rebellion. We are conditioned to believe that our worth is measured by how much we accomplish, how quickly we can complete tasks, and how many items we can check off our to-do lists. However, this relentless pursuit of productivity can leave us feeling stressed, burned out, and disconnected from our own humanity.

The slow lane invites us to challenge this pervasive mindset and to question the assumptions that underpin our fast-paced lives. It encourages us to pause, reflect, and consider what truly matters to us. It's about reclaiming our time and energy from the endless demands of the modern world and directing them towards activities that nourish our souls and bring us joy.

Embracing a slower pace can manifest in various ways. It might involve spending more time in nature, savoring a home-cooked meal, engaging in creative pursuits, or simply taking a leisurely walk. It's about prioritizing quality over quantity, depth over breadth, and presence over productivity.

Mindfulness is a key component of the slow lane. It's the practice of paying full attention to the present moment without judgment. By cultivating mindfulness, we can become more aware of our thoughts, emotions, and sensations, and develop a deeper appreciation for the simple joys of life. Whether it's savoring the taste of a cup of tea, noticing the warmth of the sun on our skin, or listening attentively to a loved one, mindfulness allows us to fully engage with the present moment and experience life more fully.

The benefits of embracing a slower, more mindful pace are numerous and profound. Research has shown that slowing down can reduce stress, improve sleep, enhance creativity, and boost overall well-being. It can also deepen our relationships, strengthen our connection with nature, and foster a greater sense of gratitude and contentment.

In a world that is constantly accelerating, the slow lane offers a refuge of tranquility and renewal. It's a place where we can recharge our batteries, reconnect with our inner selves, and cultivate a more meaningful and fulfilling life. It's an invitation to step off the hamster wheel of busyness and embrace a life that is slower, simpler, and more in tune with our natural rhythms.

The slow lane is not a destination, but a journey. It's an ongoing process of learning to let go of the need for speed and to embrace the present moment with open arms. It's about cultivating a sense of peace and tranquility amidst the chaos of modern life. As we slow down and embrace a more mindful pace, we open ourselves up to a world of beauty, joy, and wonder that is often hidden in plain sight.

Setting boundaries is an act of self-love. It's about honoring your needs, protecting your energy, and saying "no" with grace and compassion. Remember, you cannot pour from an empty cup.

SIX

The Roots of Wisdom: Learning from Ancient Traditions and Timeless Truths

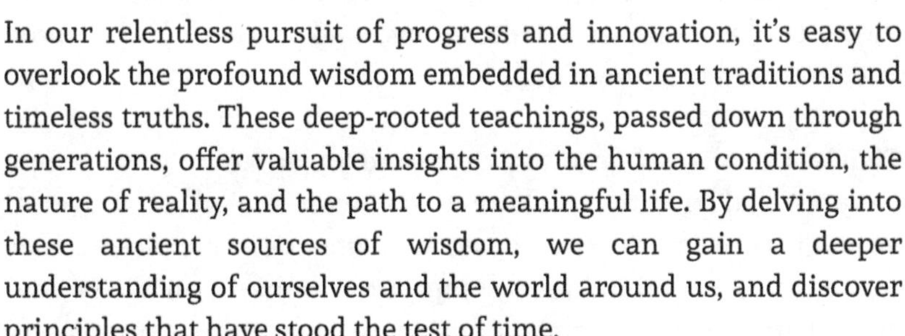

In our relentless pursuit of progress and innovation, it's easy to overlook the profound wisdom embedded in ancient traditions and timeless truths. These deep-rooted teachings, passed down through generations, offer valuable insights into the human condition, the nature of reality, and the path to a meaningful life. By delving into these ancient sources of wisdom, we can gain a deeper understanding of ourselves and the world around us, and discover principles that have stood the test of time.

Ancient traditions encompass a vast array of cultures and philosophies, each with its unique perspectives and insights. From the spiritual teachings of Buddhism and Hinduism to the philosophical musings of ancient Greece and Rome, these traditions offer a rich tapestry of wisdom that can inform our own lives.

One of the core teachings found in many ancient traditions is the interconnectedness of all things. This principle emphasizes that we are not separate individuals, but rather interconnected threads in the vast web of life. By recognizing our interdependence with others and the natural world, we can cultivate a sense of compassion, empathy, and responsibility for our actions.

Another timeless truth found in ancient traditions is the importance of living in harmony with nature. For millennia, humans have looked to the natural world for guidance and inspiration. By observing the cycles of nature, the rhythms of the seasons, and the interconnectedness of ecosystems, we can gain a deeper understanding of our place in the world and learn to live in a more sustainable and harmonious way.

Ancient traditions also emphasize the importance of inner wisdom and self-reflection. Many cultures have developed practices such as meditation, mindfulness, and contemplation to cultivate a deeper understanding of ourselves and our place in the universe. By turning our attention inward, we can gain insights into our thoughts, emotions, and motivations, and learn to live a more authentic and meaningful life.

Timeless truths, while often expressed in different ways across cultures and traditions, share a common thread of universal wisdom. These truths encompass fundamental principles such as the importance ofkindness, compassion, honesty, integrity, and respect for others. By embodying these virtues, we can create a more just, equitable, and harmonious society.

Learning from ancient traditions and timeless truths is not about blindly adhering to outdated customs or rejecting modern knowledge. It's about recognizing the wisdom that has been passed down through generations and integrating it into our own lives in a way that is relevant and meaningful. By studying the teachings of ancient sages and philosophers, we can gain valuable insights into the human condition, the nature of reality, and the path to a meaningful life.

In a world that is constantly changing and evolving, ancient traditions and timeless truths offer a sense of grounding and stability. They remind us of the enduring values that have guided humanity for millennia and offer a compass for navigating the challenges and complexities of modern life. By embracing these ancient sources of wisdom, we can gain a deeper understanding of ourselves, our relationships, and our place in the world, and discover principles that have stood the test of time.

The wisdom of ancient traditions and timeless truths is not confined to any particular culture or religion. It's a universal heritage that belongs to all of humanity. By opening ourselves to these diverse sources of wisdom, we can enrich our lives, broaden our perspectives, and cultivate a deeper sense of connection with the world around us.

Cultivate self-compassion, for it is the foundation of inner peace. Treat yourself with kindness and understanding, forgiving your mistakes and embracing your imperfections.

♡♡♡

SEVEN

Connecting with Nature: Finding Solace and Inspiration in the Natural World

In our modern, technology-driven lives, the profound connection we share with nature is often overlooked or undervalued. Yet, the natural world offers a timeless source of solace, inspiration, and rejuvenation for the human spirit. From the majestic mountains to the tranquil forests, the vast oceans to the vibrant meadows, nature beckons us to step outside our concrete jungles and rediscover our innate connection to the Earth.

Connecting with nature is not merely a leisurely pastime; it's a fundamental human need. Throughout history, humans have sought refuge, sustenance, and inspiration in the natural world. Our ancestors lived in close harmony with the Earth, attuned to its rhythms and cycles. They understood that nature was not separate from them, but rather an integral part of their existence.

In our modern lives, we have become increasingly disconnected from nature. We spend most of our time indoors, surrounded by technology and artificial environments. This disconnect has taken a toll on our physical, mental, and emotional well-being. Studies have shown that spending time in nature can reduce stress, improve mood, boost creativity, and enhance overall health.

One of the most profound benefits of connecting with nature is the sense of solace it provides. In a world that is often chaotic and overwhelming, nature offers a refuge of peace and tranquility. The gentle rustling of leaves, the soothing sound of waves crashing on the shore, the vibrant colors of a blooming flower – these simple yet profound experiences can calm our minds, soothe our souls, and restore our sense of balance.

Nature also serves as a wellspring of inspiration. Artists, writers, musicians, and thinkers throughout history have drawn inspiration from the natural world. The intricate patterns of a seashell, the majestic flight of a bird, the vibrant colors of a sunset – these natural wonders ignite our imaginations and spark our creativity. By immersing ourselves in nature, we open ourselves up to new ideas, perspectives, and possibilities.

Connecting with nature can also deepen our sense of wonder and awe. When we witness the vastness of the ocean, the towering heights of a mountain range, or the intricate details of a butterfly's wing, we are reminded of the immense beauty and complexity of the universe. This sense of awe can inspire us to live more meaningful lives, to appreciate the preciousness of life, and to strive for a greater understanding of our place in the world.

Beyond its aesthetic and inspirational qualities, nature also provides a vital connection to our own bodies and senses. In nature, we are invited to engage with the world through all our senses – to feel the earth beneath our feet, to smell the fragrance of wildflowers, to taste the sweetness of ripe berries, to hear the songs of birds, and to see the vibrant colors of a blooming landscape. This sensory immersion can awaken our bodies and minds, and reconnect us with the primal rhythms of life.

In a world that is increasingly urbanized and industrialized, it's more important than ever to make a conscious effort to connect with nature. Whether it's spending time in a local park, hiking in the mountains, swimming in the ocean, or simply tending to a backyard garden, the benefits of immersing ourselves in nature are undeniable. By reconnecting with the natural world, we can find solace, inspiration, and rejuvenation for our bodies, minds, and spirits.

Live with integrity, aligning your actions with your values and beliefs. It's not always easy, but it's the only way to live a life that is truly authentic and fulfilling.

EIGHT

The Power of Intuition: Honoring your Inner Voice and Gut Feelings

In a world saturated with information and opinions, where decisions often seem complex and overwhelming, the power of intuition emerges as a guiding light. It's that quiet whisper within us, that gut feeling that nudges us towards a certain path, that instinctive knowing that defies logic and reason. While often dismissed as mere superstition or irrationality, intuition holds a profound wisdom that can lead us to clarity, insight, and ultimately, a deeper understanding of ourselves and the world around us.

Intuition is not a mystical or supernatural phenomenon; it's a natural human faculty that arises from the depths of our unconscious mind. It's a culmination of our accumulated experiences, knowledge, and observations, processed and synthesized in ways that often elude our conscious awareness. When we tap into our intuition, we tap into a vast reservoir of wisdom that can guide us through life's challenges and uncertainties.

Honoring our inner voice and gut feelings requires us to cultivate a deep sense of self-trust. It means recognizing that we possess an innate wisdom that can guide us towards the right decisions, even when those decisions seem to defy logic or conventional wisdom. It means learning to listen to the subtle whispers of our intuition, even when they are drowned out by the noise of external opinions and expectations.

One of the most powerful ways to access our intuition is through stillness and silence. In our fast-paced, hyper-connected world, it's easy to become overwhelmed by the constant barrage of information and stimuli. By creating space for quiet reflection, meditation, or simply spending time in nature, we can tune into the subtle whispers of our intuition and gain clarity on our path.

Intuition often speaks to us through our bodies. A knot in our stomach, a tingling sensation in our spine, a sudden surge of energy – these physical sensations can be powerful signals from our intuition, guiding us towards or away from certain choices or situations. By learning to pay attention to these bodily cues, we can tap into a deeper level of knowing that goes beyond rational thought.

Intuition is not infallible, and it's important to discern between genuine intuitive guidance and our own fears, desires, or biases. This requires a willingness to be honest with ourselves, to question our assumptions, and to examine the underlying motivations behind our choices. By cultivating self-awareness and discernment, we can learn to distinguish between the true voice of our intuition and the chatter of our ego.

Honoring our intuition doesn't mean blindly following our gut feelings without any consideration for logic or reason. It's about finding a balance between our intuitive wisdom and our rational mind. By integrating these two aspects of ourselves, we can make decisions that are both informed and aligned with our deepest values and aspirations.

The power of intuition is not limited to personal decision-making. It can also be a valuable tool in our relationships, careers, and creative pursuits. By trusting our intuition, we can build stronger connections with others, make more authentic choices in our work, and tap into our creative potential.

Intuition is a gift that is available to all of us. By cultivating a deeper connection with our inner voice and honoring our gut feelings, we can tap into a wellspring of wisdom that can guide us towards a more fulfilling and purposeful life.

Simplify your relationships, focusing on those that uplift and nourish you. Let go of toxic connections that drain your energy and dim your light.

♡♡♡

NINE

Cultivating Mindfulness: Being present in the moment, with open awareness

In our modern, fast-paced world, our minds are often consumed by a whirlwind of thoughts, worries, and distractions. We rush from one task to another, constantly planning for the future or dwelling on the past, rarely pausing to fully experience the present moment. This relentless mental chatter can lead to stress, anxiety, and a sense of disconnection from ourselves and the world around us. Cultivating mindfulness offers a powerful antidote to this frenetic pace, inviting us to slow down, tune in, and embrace the richness of the present moment with open awareness.

At its core, mindfulness is the practice of paying full attention to the present moment without judgment. It involves observing our thoughts, emotions, and sensations with a gentle, non-reactive awareness. It's about being fully present in our bodies, our minds, and our surroundings, without getting caught up in the stories we tell ourselves or the judgments we make.

Mindfulness is not about emptying our minds or achieving a state of blissful detachment. It's about acknowledging and accepting whatever arises in our experience, whether it's pleasant or unpleasant, without trying to change it or push it away. By cultivating this open, non-judgmental awareness, we can learn to relate to our thoughts and emotions with greater clarity and compassion.

One of the most powerful ways to cultivate mindfulness is through meditation. By setting aside time each day to sit in silence and observe our breath, we can train our minds to become more focused, calm, and present. As we meditate, we may notice that our minds wander to thoughts about the past or future, or to worries and anxieties. This is perfectly normal. The key is to gently bring our attention back to the present moment, without judgment or criticism.

Mindfulness is not limited to formal meditation practice. It can be integrated into our daily lives, infusing every moment with greater awareness and presence. We can practice mindfulness while walking, eating, washing dishes, or even brushing our teeth. By paying attention to the sensations of our bodies, the sights and sounds around us, and the thoughts and emotions that arise, we can cultivate a more mindful way of being.

The benefits of mindfulness are numerous and far-reaching. Research has shown that mindfulness can reduce stress, anxiety, and depression, improve sleep, enhance focus and concentration, and boost overall well-being. It can also help us to develop greater self-awareness, compassion, and resilience in the face of life's challenges.

By cultivating mindfulness, we can learn to break free from the autopilot mode that often governs our lives. We can become more aware of our habitual patterns of thinking and behavior, and make conscious choices that align with our values and goals. We can learn to respond to life's challenges with greater equanimity, rather than reacting impulsively or getting caught up in negative emotions.

Mindfulness is not a quick fix or a magic bullet. It's a lifelong journey of self-discovery and growth. By committing to a regular mindfulness practice, we can cultivate a deeper connection to ourselves, our loved ones, and the world around us. We can learn to live more fully, more authentically, and more joyfully in each moment.

Find purpose in your work and life, a guiding star that ignites your passion and fuels your soul. It's not just about what you do, but why you do it.

♡♡♡

TEN

The Practice of Gratitude: Acknowledging and Appreciating Life's Blessings

In a world often consumed by the pursuit of more, the practice of gratitude offers a refreshing and transformative perspective. It's a conscious choice to shift our focus from what we lack to what we have, to acknowledge and appreciate the countless blessings that enrich our lives. Gratitude is not merely a fleeting emotion; it's a way of life, a mindset that can profoundly impact our well-being and happiness.

At its core, gratitude is a deep appreciation for the goodness in our lives. It's a recognition that we are not entitled to the good things that come our way, but rather, that they are gifts to be cherished. Whether it's the love of family and friends, the beauty of nature, the simple pleasures of a good meal, or the opportunities that life presents us, gratitude invites us to pause and acknowledge the abundance that surrounds us.

The practice of gratitude is not about denying the challenges and difficulties we face in life. It's about acknowledging the good alongside the bad, and finding reasons to be thankful even in the midst of adversity. Gratitude is not a form of denial or wishful thinking; it's a realistic and grounded approach to life that allows us to see the full spectrum of human experience.

One of the most powerful ways to cultivate gratitude is through daily reflection. By taking a few moments each day to reflect on the things we are thankful for, we can train our minds to focus on the positive aspects of our lives. This can be as simple as jotting down three things we are grateful for in a gratitude journal, sharing our appreciation with a loved one, or simply taking a moment to silently acknowledge the blessings we have received.

Gratitude is not just a personal practice; it's also a social act. When we express our gratitude to others, we not only brighten their day but also strengthen our relationships. A simple "thank you" can go a long way in showing appreciation for the people in our lives and fostering a sense of connection and goodwill.

The benefits of practicing gratitude are numerous and far-reaching. Research has shown that gratitude can improve our physical and mental health, reduce stress and anxiety, boost self-esteem, enhance resilience, and even improve our sleep. Gratitude can also have a positive impact on our relationships, making us more compassionate, empathetic, and forgiving.

By cultivating gratitude, we can shift our perspective from one of lack to one of abundance. We begin to see the world through a lens of possibility and opportunity, rather than scarcity and limitation. We become more attuned to the good things in our lives, and less focused on what we are missing. This shift in perspective can have a profound impact on our overall happiness and well-being.

Gratitude is not a passive state; it's an active choice we make every day. It requires us to be mindful of our thoughts and emotions, to notice the good that surrounds us, and to express our appreciation for the blessings we have received. By making gratitude a daily practice, we can transform our lives from the inside out, cultivating a deeper sense of joy, peace, and contentment.

In a world that often encourages us to focus on what we lack, the practice of gratitude is a radical act of self-love. It's a choice to embrace the abundance that already exists in our lives, and to cultivate a heart full of thankfulness for the gifts we have been given.

Resilience is the art of bouncing back, of finding strength in adversity. Embrace challenges as opportunities for growth, and remember that setbacks are merely stepping stones to success.

ELEVEN

The Courage to Be Yourself: Embracing your uniqueness and letting go of comparison

In our modern, image-driven society, we're constantly bombarded with messages telling us how to look, behave, and achieve success. This can lead to a sense of inadequacy and a desire to conform to unrealistic standards of beauty and perfection. However, embracing your uniqueness and letting go of comparison is essential for living a fulfilling and authentic life.

The courage to be yourself is a lifelong journey of self-discovery and self-acceptance. It's about recognizing and honoring your unique gifts, talents, and quirks, and embracing the totality of who you are, flaws and all. It's about letting go of the need to fit in or conform to societal expectations, and instead, choosing to live a life that is true to your own values, passions, and aspirations.

Comparison is a natural human tendency. We often compare ourselves to others in terms of appearance, achievements, possessions, and even happiness. However, comparison can be a double-edged sword. While it can motivate us to strive for improvement, it can also lead to feelings of inadequacy, envy, and self-doubt. When we constantly compare ourselves to others, we lose sight of our own unique value and potential.

Embracing your uniqueness starts with self-acceptance. It's about recognizing that you are a one-of-a-kind individual with your own strengths, weaknesses, and imperfections. It's about learning to love and accept yourself for who you are, not who you think you should be. When you embrace your uniqueness, you free yourself from the need to conform to external standards and open yourself up to a world of possibilities.

Letting go of comparison requires a conscious effort to shift our focus from others to ourselves. It's about recognizing that everyone has their own journey, their own challenges, and their own timeline. It's about celebrating our own successes and learning from our own failures, without comparing ourselves to others. When we let go of comparison, we free ourselves from the tyranny of external validation and open ourselves up to a deeper sense of inner peace and contentment.

Embracing your uniqueness and letting go of comparison can be a challenging process, but it's also incredibly liberating. When you stop trying to be someone you're not, you free up energy that can be used to pursue your passions, cultivate your talents, and make a meaningful contribution to the world. You also become a role model for others, inspiring them to embrace their own unique qualities and live authentic lives.

To cultivate the courage to be yourself, start by practicing self-compassion. Treat yourself with the same kindness and understanding that you would offer to a close friend. When you make mistakes, instead of beating yourself up, acknowledge your shortcomings with grace and learn from them. When you feel insecure or inadequate, remind yourself of your strengths and accomplishments.

Another powerful way to embrace your uniqueness is to surround yourself with people who support and encourage you to be your authentic self. Seek out relationships with people who celebrate your individuality, challenge you to grow, and inspire you to be the best version of yourself.

Remember that embracing your uniqueness is not about being perfect. It's about being real, honest, and vulnerable. It's about accepting your flaws and imperfections, and recognizing that they are part of what makes you unique and beautiful.

In a world that often values conformity, the courage to be yourself is a radical act of self-love. It's a choice to live a life that is true to your own values, passions, and aspirations, regardless of what others think or expect of you. By embracing your uniqueness and letting go of comparison, you open yourself up to a world of possibilities and create a life that is truly your own.

Embrace the journey, for it is in the journey that we discover our true selves. Let simplicity, wisdom, and authenticity be your guiding lights.

♡♡♡

TWELVE

Finding Your Voice: Speaking your Truth with Confidence and Compassion

In a world filled with diverse perspectives and competing narratives, finding your voice and speaking your truth can be a transformative and empowering experience. It's about discovering and expressing your authentic self, sharing your thoughts, feelings, and beliefs with confidence and compassion. While it may seem daunting at first, finding your voice is a journey of self-discovery that can lead to greater self-awareness, deeper connections with others, and a more meaningful life.

Finding your voice begins with self-reflection and introspection. It requires taking the time to explore your values, beliefs, and passions. What is important to you? What do you stand for? What are your unique experiences and perspectives? By delving into these questions, you can begin to uncover the core of your being and identify the truths that resonate most deeply within you.

Speaking your truth is not just about expressing your opinions or views; it's about sharing your authentic self with the world. It's about communicating from a place of vulnerability and honesty, even when it feels uncomfortable or risky. It's about being willing to stand up for what you believe in, even when it goes against the grain.

Confidence is a key ingredient in finding and expressing your voice. It's about believing in yourself and your message, even when faced with doubt or opposition. Confidence is not about arrogance or ego; it's about knowing your worth and trusting in your ability to make a positive impact. When you speak with confidence, you inspire others to listen and engage with your message.

Compassion is equally important in speaking your truth. It's about recognizing that everyone has their own unique experiences and perspectives, and that we can learn from each other by listening with an open mind and heart. Compassion is about understanding that our words can have a profound impact on others, and that we should always strive to communicate with kindness, empathy, and respect.

Finding your voice is not a one-time event; it's an ongoing process of self-discovery and growth. As we evolve and change, so too does our understanding of ourselves and the world around us. This means that our voice may also evolve over time, reflecting our changing perspectives and experiences.

One of the most powerful ways to find your voice is through creative expression. Whether it's writing, painting, music, or any other form of art, creative expression allows us to tap into our emotions, explore our inner world, and communicate our truths in a unique and meaningful way. By engaging in creative expression, we can unlock hidden depths within ourselves and discover new ways of expressing our authentic selves.

Another important aspect of finding your voice is building a supportive community. Surround yourself with people who encourage you to be your authentic self, who listen to your ideas with respect, and who challenge you to grow and evolve. A supportive community can provide a safe space for you to explore your voice, share your experiences, and receive feedback and encouragement.

It's also important to remember that finding your voice is not about seeking approval or validation from others. It's about staying true to yourself, even when faced with criticism or rejection. Ultimately, the most important audience for your voice is yourself. When you speak your truth with confidence and compassion, you honor your own authenticity and contribute to a more honest and meaningful dialogue in the world.

The slow lane is a sanctuary for the soul. It's a place to recharge, reconnect with nature, and savor the simple joys of life. Slow down, breathe deeply, and be present in the moment.

THIRTEEN

Setting Boundaries: Protecting your Energy and Saying "No" when Necessary

In our interconnected world, where demands on our time and energy are ever-present, the art of setting boundaries emerges as an essential practice for self-preservation and well-being. Boundaries are the invisible lines we draw to define our limits, protect our energy, and maintain a healthy balance in our relationships and lives. While often perceived as selfish or confrontational, setting boundaries is a powerful act of self-love and respect, allowing us to honor our needs, prioritize our well-being, and cultivate healthier connections with others.

At its core, setting boundaries is about knowing and honoring our limits. It's about recognizing that we cannot be everything to everyone, and that it's okay to say no when necessary. Boundaries can encompass various aspects of our lives, including our time, energy, emotions, physical space, and even our values and beliefs. They serve as a protective shield, allowing us to conserve our resources and maintain a sense of personal autonomy.

One of the most challenging aspects of setting boundaries is learning to say no. We are often conditioned to be people-pleasers, to prioritize the needs of others over our own, and to avoid conflict at all costs. However, this can lead to resentment, burnout, and a loss of our own identity. By learning to say no, we reclaim our power and autonomy, and we send a clear message that we value our own well-being.

Setting boundaries is not about being selfish or rejecting others. It's about establishing healthy limits that allow us to show up fully in our relationships and commitments. When we have clear boundaries, we are better able to give our time and energy to the things that truly matter to us, without feeling overwhelmed or depleted.

It's important to remember that boundaries are not static. They can evolve and change over time, depending on our circumstances and needs. What worked for us in the past may not be appropriate for us now. It's important to regularly check in with ourselves and reassess our boundaries, ensuring that they continue to serve our best interests.

Setting boundaries can be challenging, especially in relationships where there is a power imbalance or a history of codependency. It may require difficult conversations, uncomfortable emotions, and even a re-evaluation of certain relationships. However, the long-term benefits of setting boundaries far outweigh the short-term discomfort.

To set effective boundaries, it's important to be clear and assertive in our communication. This means expressing our needs and limits in a direct and respectful way, without apologizing or making excuses. It also means being willing to enforce our boundaries, even when faced with resistance or pushback.

Remember that setting boundaries is not a one-time event; it's an ongoing practice. It requires constant vigilance and a willingness to re-evaluate our choices on a regular basis. However, the rewards are immeasurable. By setting boundaries, we protect our energy, prioritize our well-being, and cultivate healthier relationships with ourselves and others.

In a world that constantly demands our attention and energy, the ability to set boundaries is a superpower. It allows us to navigate the complexities of life with grace and resilience, while honoring our own needs and values. By embracing the art of setting boundaries, we empower ourselves to live a life that is authentic, fulfilling, and truly our own.

Gratitude is the key to abundance. Acknowledge and appreciate the blessings in your life, no matter how small. A grateful heart is a magnet for joy and abundance.

♡♡♡

FOURTEEN

The Art of Self-Compassion: Treating yourself with kindness and understanding

In a world that often emphasizes self-criticism and harsh judgment, the art of self-compassion emerges as a radical act of kindness and self-care. It's a way of relating to ourselves with the same warmth, understanding, and acceptance that we would offer to a dear friend or loved one. Self-compassion is not about self-indulgence or self-pity; it's about recognizing our common humanity and embracing our imperfections with kindness and understanding.

At its core, self-compassion involves three key elements: self-kindness, common humanity, and mindfulness. Self-kindness means treating ourselves with the same warmth and understanding that we would offer to a friend who is struggling. It means recognizing that we are all human, and that we all make mistakes, experience setbacks, and face challenges. It means offering ourselves words of encouragement and support, rather than criticism and judgment.

Common humanity reminds us that we are not alone in our struggles. Everyone experiences pain, suffering, and imperfection. When we recognize this shared human experience, we can let go of the isolating feeling that we are somehow flawed or defective. Instead, we can connect with others on a deeper level, offering and receiving compassion and support.

Mindfulness is the practice of paying attention to the present moment without judgment. It involves observing our thoughts and emotions with a gentle, non-reactive awareness. When we are mindful, we can recognize when we are being self-critical or engaging in negative self-talk, and we can choose to respond with kindness and compassion instead.

The practice of self-compassion is not always easy. We may have deeply ingrained patterns of self-criticism and negative self-talk that are difficult to break. However, with practice and patience, we can learn to cultivate a more compassionate relationship with ourselves.

One way to cultivate self-compassion is to start by noticing when we are being self-critical. When we catch ourselves engaging in negative self-talk, we can pause and ask ourselves, "Would I speak to a friend this way?" If the answer is no, we can choose to reframe our thoughts in a more compassionate and supportive way.

Another way to practice self-compassion is to engage in activities that nourish our bodies and minds. This might include exercise, spending time in nature, practicing relaxation techniques, or engaging in creative pursuits. By taking care of ourselves, we are sending a message to ourselves that we are worthy of love and care.

Self-compassion is not a one-time event; it's an ongoing practice. It requires us to be mindful of our thoughts and emotions, and to choose kindness and understanding over judgment and criticism. With time and practice, self-compassion can become a way of life, transforming our relationship with ourselves and leading to greater happiness, resilience, and well-being.

The benefits of self-compassion are numerous and far-reaching. Research has shown that self-compassion can reduce stress, anxiety, and depression, improve self-esteem, enhance resilience, and even improve our physical health. It can also help us to cultivate healthier relationships, as we learn to extend compassion to others as well as ourselves.

In a world that often tells us that we are not enough, the art of self-compassion is a radical act of self-love. It's a choice to embrace our imperfections, to forgive ourselves for our mistakes, and to treat ourselves with the same kindness and understanding that we would offer to a dear friend. By cultivating self-compassion, we can create a more peaceful, joyful, and fulfilling life for ourselves and those around us.

Embrace the natural world, for it is a source of solace, inspiration, and healing. Let the beauty of nature fill your senses and ignite your creativity.

♡♡♡

FIFTEEN

Living with Integrity: Aligning Your Actions with Your Values and Beliefs

In an era of fleeting trends and shifting values, living with integrity stands as a timeless principle that guides individuals toward a life of authenticity and purpose. Integrity is the unwavering commitment to align our actions with our deeply held values and beliefs, even when faced with challenges, temptations, or external pressures. It is the foundation upon which trust, respect, and genuine relationships are built, and it empowers us to live a life that is both meaningful and fulfilling.

At its core, integrity is about being true to oneself. It involves a deep understanding of our values, the guiding principles that shape our worldview and determine our priorities. When we live with integrity, our actions reflect these values, creating a sense of congruence between our inner and outer worlds. This alignment fosters a sense of peace, authenticity, and fulfillment, as we live in accordance with our deepest convictions.

Living with integrity requires courage and resilience. In a world that often rewards compromise and conformity, staying true to our values can be a challenging endeavor. We may face situations where our values are tested, where we are tempted to take the easy way out or to prioritize personal gain over ethical considerations. It is in these moments that our integrity is truly revealed.

Integrity is not about being perfect or never making mistakes. We are all human, and we all stumble at times. The key is to acknowledge our shortcomings, learn from them, and recommit to our values. When we make mistakes, integrity calls us to take responsibility for our actions, apologize if necessary, and strive to do better in the future.

Integrity is not just a personal virtue; it has far-reaching implications for our relationships, communities, and society as a whole. When we live with integrity, we build trust with others. People know that they can rely on us to be honest, dependable, and consistent in our words and actions. This trust is the foundation for strong and lasting relationships, both personal and professional.

Integrity also plays a crucial role in our communities and society. When individuals act with integrity, it creates a ripple effect that can inspire others to do the same. It fosters a culture of honesty, accountability, and ethical behavior, which benefits everyone. Conversely, a lack of integrity can erode trust, create division, and undermine the very fabric of society.

Living with integrity is not always easy, but it is always worthwhile.

It requires us to be mindful of our choices, to reflect on our values, and to make decisions that are in alignment with our deepest convictions. It challenges us to be courageous in the face of adversity, to stand up for what we believe in, and to speak our truth, even when it's unpopular.

The rewards of living with integrity are immeasurable. It brings a sense of peace, knowing that we are living in alignment with our values. It fosters authentic relationships built on trust and respect. It empowers us to make a positive impact on the world, as our actions inspire others to do the same.

In a world that is constantly changing and evolving, living with integrity provides a stable foundation upon which we can build our lives. It is a guiding principle that transcends cultural boundaries and temporal constraints, offering a timeless path to a life of meaning, purpose, and fulfillment.

Find your voice and speak your truth with confidence and compassion. Your words have power, so use them to uplift, inspire, and create positive change.

♡♡♡

SIXTEEN

SIMPLIFYING RELATIONSHIPS: FOSTERING MEANINGFUL CONNECTIONS AND LETTING GO OF TOXIC ONES

In our complex and interconnected lives, relationships play a pivotal role in shaping our happiness, well-being, and overall quality of life. However, not all relationships are created equal. Some uplift and nourish us, while others drain our energy, create conflict, and hinder our personal growth. Simplifying relationships is the art of fostering meaningful connections while recognizing and letting go of toxic ones, creating space for healthier, more fulfilling interactions.

Meaningful connections are the cornerstone of a happy and fulfilling life. They provide us with love, support, and a sense of belonging. These relationships are characterized by mutual respect, trust, open communication, and shared values. They enrich our lives, challenge us to grow, and provide a safe haven where we can be our authentic selves.

Fostering meaningful connections requires effort, intentionality, and a willingness to be vulnerable. It involves actively listening to others, showing empathy and understanding, and expressing our own thoughts and feelings openly and honestly. It also involves being present in the moment, truly engaging with the people we care about, and making time for shared experiences and meaningful conversations.

In a world that is constantly vying for our attention, nurturing meaningful connections can be a challenge. We are often bombarded with distractions, from the constant pings of our smartphones to the never-ending demands of work and social obligations. To create space for deeper connections, we need to be intentional about how we spend our time and energy. This may involve setting boundaries with technology, scheduling regular time for meaningful conversations with loved ones, or simply being present in the moment when we are with others.

While fostering meaningful connections is essential, it's equally important to recognize and let go of toxic relationships. Toxic relationships are those that consistently leave us feeling drained, devalued, or emotionally wounded. They may involve manipulation, control, criticism, or a lack of respect. These relationships can have a detrimental impact on our mental, emotional, and even physical health.

Recognizing toxic relationships can be difficult, especially if we have been invested in them for a long time. We may feel a sense of loyalty, obligation, or even guilt. However, it's important to remember that we deserve to be treated with respect and kindness. If a relationship consistently brings us more pain than joy, it may be time to let it go.

Letting go of toxic relationships doesn't mean that we are abandoning the person or that we don't care about them. It means that we are prioritizing our own well-being and creating space for healthier connections. It may involve setting boundaries, limiting contact, or even ending the relationship altogether. While this can be a painful process, it's ultimately a liberating one, as it frees us from the negative energy and emotional drain of a toxic relationship.

Simplifying relationships is an ongoing process. It requires us to be mindful of our interactions with others, to pay attention to how we feel in their presence, and to make conscious choices about the relationships we cultivate. It's about prioritizing the relationships that uplift and nourish us, while letting go of those that no longer serve us.

By simplifying our relationships, we create space for deeper connections, greater joy, and more fulfilling interactions. We free ourselves from the burden of toxic relationships and open ourselves up to the possibility of new and meaningful connections that can enrich our lives in countless ways.

ÞÞÞ

Let go of the need for external validation. True happiness and fulfillment come from within, from a deep sense of self-worth and self-acceptance.

♡♡♡

SEVENTEEN

The Pursuit of Purpose: Finding Meaning and Fulfillment in Your Work and Life

In the tapestry of human existence, the pursuit of purpose is a universal thread, woven into the fabric of our lives. It's a yearning for meaning, a desire to make a difference, and a quest to find fulfillment in our work and lives. While the concept of purpose may seem elusive and abstract, it holds the key to unlocking our full potential and living a life of deep satisfaction and significance.

The pursuit of purpose is not merely about finding a job or career that we enjoy; it's about discovering a deeper sense of meaning and contribution in everything we do. It's about aligning our actions with our values, passions, and talents, and using our unique gifts to make a positive impact on the world. When we live a life of purpose, we feel a sense of direction, motivation, and fulfillment that goes beyond material success or external recognition.

Finding our purpose is a journey of self-discovery. It requires us to delve deep within ourselves and explore our passions, interests, and values. It involves asking ourselves fundamental questions about what we care about, what we are good at, and how we can use our unique skills and talents to make a difference. It's a process of exploration, experimentation, and reflection, where we may try different paths, learn from our experiences, and gradually refine our understanding of our purpose.

Purpose is not a static concept; it can evolve and change throughout our lives. Our passions, interests, and priorities may shift as we gain new experiences and perspectives. The pursuit of purpose is therefore not a one-time event, but an ongoing process of self-discovery and growth.

The pursuit of purpose is not limited to our work lives; it encompasses every aspect of our existence. While finding meaning and fulfillment in our careers is important, it's equally important to find purpose in our relationships, hobbies, community involvement, and personal growth. When we live a life of purpose, we integrate our values and passions into every facet of our lives, creating a sense of wholeness and coherence.

Finding our purpose can be a challenging journey, filled with doubts, setbacks, and uncertainties. We may encounter obstacles, face criticism or rejection, or feel lost and directionless at times. However, it's precisely in these moments of challenge that our purpose can shine through. By persevering in the face of adversity, we can discover our inner strength, resilience, and determination.

The pursuit of purpose is not a solo endeavor. We can find guidance and support from mentors, friends, family, and communities. By sharing our aspirations, seeking feedback, and learning from the experiences of others, we can gain valuable insights and direction on our journey.

Ultimately, the pursuit of purpose is a deeply personal and individualistic endeavor. There is no one-size-fits-all answer, no single path that will lead everyone to fulfillment. Each of us must discover our own unique purpose, based on our individual talents, passions, and values.

The rewards of living a life of purpose are immeasurable. It brings a sense of meaning, joy, and fulfillment that goes beyond material success or external recognition. It gives us a sense of direction and purpose, motivating us to overcome challenges and strive for our goals. It allows us to connect with others on a deeper level, as we share our passions and work towards common goals.

In a world that often values material success and external validation, the pursuit of purpose offers a refreshing alternative. It invites us to look beyond the superficial and focus on what truly matters - our values, our passions, and our contributions to the world. By embracing our unique purpose, we can create a life that is both meaningful and fulfilling.

Live each day with intention, focusing on what truly matters. Let go of distractions and busyness, and create a life that is aligned with your values and priorities.

♡♡♡

EIGHTEEN

Thriving in Uncertainty: Embracing Change and Adapting to New Challenges

In the rapidly evolving landscape of the 21st century, uncertainty has become a constant companion. Whether in personal lives, professional environments, or societal contexts, change is inevitable. The ability to thrive in uncertainty is not just a desirable skill but a crucial one. Thriving in uncertainty requires a multifaceted approach that encompasses psychological resilience, social adaptability, and practical strategies for navigating the unknown.

Uncertainty is often perceived as a negative state, associated with fear, anxiety, and a lack of control. It is essential to recognize that uncertainty also presents opportunities for growth, innovation, and transformation. Change can disrupt established routines and comfort zones, but it also fosters resilience, adaptability, and progress. The human brain is wired to seek patterns and predictability. When faced with uncertainty, the brain's natural response is to trigger stress reactions, perceiving potential threats. This evolutionary mechanism, while useful for survival in ancient times, can hinder our ability to cope with modern-day challenges.

The first step towards thriving in uncertainty is to reframe our perspective. Instead of viewing uncertainty as a threat, we can see it as a realm of possibilities. Embracing a growth mindset is crucial in this process. A growth mindset, as opposed to a fixed mindset, allows individuals to see challenges as opportunities to learn and improve. This shift in perspective can significantly reduce the anxiety associated with uncertainty and open up new avenues for personal and professional development.

Adaptability is another key component of thriving in uncertainty. Adaptability involves being flexible and open to new experiences and ideas. It requires a willingness to step out of one's comfort zone and take risks. In a rapidly changing world, those who can adapt quickly to new circumstances are more likely to succeed. This adaptability can be cultivated through continuous learning and development. Staying informed about trends and advancements in one's field, acquiring new skills, and being open to feedback are all ways to enhance adaptability.

Resilience is the ability to bounce back from adversity. It is a critical quality for thriving in uncertain times. Building resilience involves developing coping strategies to manage stress and adversity. This can include maintaining a positive outlook, finding meaning and purpose in difficult situations, and fostering strong social connections. Support from family, friends, and colleagues can provide a buffer against the negative effects of stress and help individuals navigate through challenging times.

Effective decision-making is also essential for thriving in uncertainty. In uncertain situations, it is often necessary to make decisions with incomplete information. This requires a balance of intuition and rational analysis. Intuition, or gut feeling, is informed by experience and can be a valuable tool in decision-making. However, it should be complemented by a thorough analysis of available data and potential outcomes. Developing a structured approach to decision-making, such as weighing pros and cons or using decision matrices, can help mitigate the risks associated with uncertainty.

Another important aspect of thriving in uncertainty is embracing change. Change is often met with resistance because it disrupts the status quo and introduces unfamiliar elements. However, embracing change means recognizing its potential benefits and actively seeking out opportunities for growth and improvement. This can involve setting new goals, experimenting with different approaches, and being proactive in driving change rather than merely reacting to it.

In addition to personal resilience and adaptability, thriving in uncertainty also requires effective leadership. Leaders play a crucial role in guiding their teams through uncertain times. Effective leaders are those who can inspire confidence, provide clear direction, and foster a culture of innovation and collaboration. They must be able to communicate effectively, build trust, and empower their team members to take initiative and contribute their ideas.

Cultivating a supportive and inclusive organizational culture is vital for navigating uncertainty. Organizations that encourage open communication, diversity of thought, and a shared sense of purpose are better equipped to handle change and uncertainty. Creating an environment where employees feel valued and respected can enhance their engagement and commitment, leading to higher levels of creativity and innovation.

On a societal level, thriving in uncertainty requires collective effort and cooperation. Societies that are resilient in the face of uncertainty are those that promote social cohesion, equity, and justice. This involves addressing systemic issues that contribute to inequality and ensuring that all individuals have access to resources and opportunities. Building resilient communities means fostering a sense of solidarity and mutual support, where individuals work together to overcome challenges and build a better future.

In the context of global challenges such as climate change, pandemics, and economic instability, thriving in uncertainty also involves a proactive and forward-thinking approach. This includes investing in research and development, implementing sustainable practices, and developing contingency plans for potential crises. Governments, businesses, and individuals all have a role to play in creating a more resilient and adaptable society.

Embracing uncertainty also means being prepared for the unexpected. This involves developing skills such as critical thinking, problem-solving, and creativity. These skills enable individuals to navigate complex and ambiguous situations, generate innovative solutions, and make informed decisions. Additionally, fostering a sense of curiosity and a willingness to explore new ideas and perspectives can lead to greater adaptability and resilience.

Thriving in uncertainty is a multifaceted endeavor that requires psychological resilience, social adaptability, and practical strategies. It involves reframing our perspective on uncertainty, embracing a growth mindset, and developing adaptability and resilience. Effective decision-making, embracing change, and fostering supportive organizational and societal cultures are also crucial. By cultivating these qualities and skills, individuals and organizations can not only survive but thrive in the face of uncertainty. Embracing change and adapting to new challenges can lead to personal and collective growth, innovation, and a brighter future.

The journey towards simplicity, wisdom, and authenticity is a lifelong process. Embrace the challenges, celebrate the victories, and trust that you are exactly where you need to be.

♡♡♡

NINETEEN

The Gift of Resilience: Bouncing Back from Setbacks and Finding Strength in Adversity

Life is an unpredictable journey filled with both triumphs and setbacks. We encounter challenges, disappointments, and even tragedies along the way. However, within each adversity lies an opportunity for growth, transformation, and the discovery of our own resilience. Resilience is the remarkable ability to bounce back from setbacks, to adapt to change, and to find strength in the face of adversity. It's a gift that allows us to navigate life's storms with grace, courage, and ultimately, emerge stronger and wiser.

Resilience is not about ignoring or denying our pain. It's about acknowledging our struggles, feeling our emotions, and then finding ways to cope, heal, and move forward. It's about recognizing that setbacks are a natural part of life, and that they can provide valuable opportunities for learning and growth.

The roots of resilience often lie in our early experiences. Children who are raised in supportive and nurturing environments, where they are encouraged to explore, learn from their mistakes, and develop a sense of self-efficacy, tend to be more resilient later in life. However, resilience is not a fixed trait; it's a skill that can be cultivated and strengthened at any age.

One of the key components of resilience is a positive mindset. When faced with adversity, resilient individuals focus on their strengths, resources, and opportunities for growth. They maintain a sense of hope and optimism, even in the darkest of times. This positive outlook allows them to see challenges as opportunities, setbacks as learning experiences, and failures as stepping stones to success.

Resilience also involves a strong sense of self-efficacy, the belief in our ability to cope with challenges and overcome obstacles. When we believe in ourselves, we are more likely to persevere in the face of adversity, to seek out solutions, and to bounce back from setbacks.

Another important aspect of resilience is social support. Having a network of supportive relationships with family, friends, or community members can provide a crucial buffer against stress and adversity. When we feel connected to others, we are more likely to seek help when we need it, to share our burdens, and to receive the emotional and practical support that can help us navigate difficult times.

Resilience is not about being invincible or immune to pain. It's about acknowledging our vulnerability, allowing ourselves to grieve, and then finding ways to heal and move forward. It's about recognizing that setbacks are not the end of the world, but rather opportunities for growth and transformation.

The gift of resilience can be cultivated through a variety of practices. Mindfulness meditation, for example, can help us to become more aware of our thoughts and emotions, allowing us to respond to challenges with greater clarity and equanimity. Physical exercise, healthy eating habits, and adequate sleep can also boost our resilience by strengthening our bodies and minds.

Resilience is a precious gift that allows us to navigate life's challenges with grace, courage, and wisdom. It's a skill that can be cultivated and strengthened through practice, self-care, and supportive relationships. By embracing our resilience, we can transform adversity into opportunity, setbacks into stepping stones, and pain into growth.

Your life is a unique and precious gift. Embrace it fully, live it passionately, and make your mark on the world.

♡♡♡

TWENTY

The Ripple Effect: Inspiring Others to Embrace Simplicity, Wisdom, and Authenticity

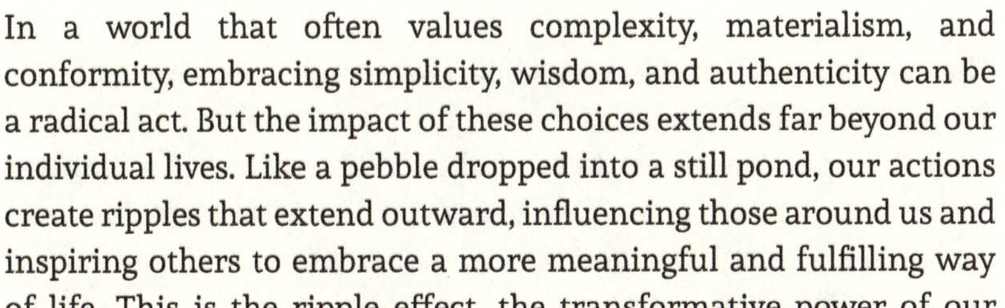

In a world that often values complexity, materialism, and conformity, embracing simplicity, wisdom, and authenticity can be a radical act. But the impact of these choices extends far beyond our individual lives. Like a pebble dropped into a still pond, our actions create ripples that extend outward, influencing those around us and inspiring others to embrace a more meaningful and fulfilling way of life. This is the ripple effect, the transformative power of our individual choices to create positive change in the world.

When we choose to simplify our lives, we send a powerful message to those around us. We demonstrate that it's possible to live a fulfilling life without being consumed by the pursuit of more. We show that happiness can be found in the simple pleasures, in meaningful connections, and in a life that is aligned with our values. By embracing simplicity, we inspire others to question the materialistic values that often dominate our culture and to consider a different path, one that prioritizes well-being, connection, and purpose.

Wisdom, the accumulated knowledge and understanding gained through experience and reflection, is a gift that we can share with others. When we share our wisdom, we offer guidance, support, and inspiration to those who are seeking their own path. We can do this through our words, our actions, and the way we live our lives. By mentoring others, volunteering our time, or simply sharing our stories and experiences, we can plant seeds of wisdom that may blossom into a lifelong love of learning and growth.

Authenticity is the courage to be ourselves, to embrace our unique quirks, passions, and perspectives. When we live authentically, we give others permission to do the same. We create a space where people feel safe to express themselves, to share their stories, and to embrace their own individuality. By living our truth, we inspire others to shed their masks, step into their own power, and live lives that are true to their own hearts.

The ripple effect is not just about inspiring others to embrace simplicity, wisdom, and authenticity; it's also about creating a positive impact on the world around us. When we live in alignment with our values, we contribute to a more compassionate, just, and sustainable society. Our actions, no matter how small, can have a profound impact on the world.

The ripple effect is a reminder that we are all interconnected. Our choices, our actions, and our words have the power to influence those around us. By choosing to live a life of simplicity, wisdom, and authenticity, we not only enrich our own lives but also create a positive ripple effect that can inspire and uplift others.

This ripple effect can be seen in countless examples throughout history. From the civil rights movement to the environmental movement, individuals who dared to live their truth and challenge the status quo have sparked movements that have changed the world. Their courage, wisdom, and authenticity have inspired others to join their cause, creating a wave of change that has swept across nations and continents.

In our own lives, the ripple effect can be seen in the small, everyday acts of kindness and generosity. When we offer a helping hand to a stranger, a listening ear to a friend, or a kind word to a colleague, we create a ripple of positivity that can spread far and wide. By choosing to live with compassion, empathy, and generosity, we create a more loving and supportive world for ourselves and others.

The ripple effect is a powerful reminder that we are not alone. We are part of a vast network of interconnected beings, all striving to live meaningful and fulfilling lives. By embracing our own uniqueness, sharing our wisdom, and living with integrity, we can inspire others to do the same, creating a ripple effect that can transform the world.

Remember, you are not alone. We are all interconnected, and our actions have a ripple effect on those around us. Choose to live a life that inspires and uplifts others.

♡♡♡

TWENTY-ONE

SUMMARY

In a world that incessantly pulls us towards complexity, excess, and the relentless pursuit of external validation, the path to a truly fulfilling life lies in embracing simplicity, wisdom, and authenticity. It is a journey of self-discovery, of peeling back the layers of societal conditioning and rediscovering our innate connection to ourselves, others, and the natural world.

The call of simplicity beckons us to declutter our lives, both physically and mentally. By letting go of the excess possessions, commitments, and distractions that weigh us down, we create space for what truly matters. We rediscover the joy of enough, finding contentment in the present moment and appreciating the simple pleasures that life has to offer.

In the slow lane, we find solace and rejuvenation. By slowing down our pace and embracing mindfulness, we become more attuned to the present moment, savoring the beauty of the world around us and cultivating a deeper connection to our own inner wisdom. It is in this stillness that we can truly hear the whispers of our intuition, guiding us towards our authentic path.

The roots of wisdom lie in the timeless truths and ancient traditions that have been passed down through generations. By learning from the wisdom of our ancestors, we can gain valuable insights into the human condition, the nature of reality, and the path to a meaningful life. We discover the interconnectedness of all things, the importance of living in harmony with nature, and the power of inner reflection.

To live authentically, we must embrace our uniqueness and let go of the need for comparison. We must have the courage to be ourselves, to express our truth with confidence and compassion, and to set healthy boundaries that protect our energy and well-being. It is in embracing our individuality that we discover our true potential and make our unique contribution to the world.

Cultivating self-compassion is essential for living a fulfilling life. By treating ourselves with kindness and understanding, we can break free from the cycle of self-criticism and negative self-talk. We learn to embrace our imperfections, forgive our mistakes, and cultivate a deep sense of self-love and acceptance.

Living with integrity is the cornerstone of a meaningful life. It means aligning our actions with our values and beliefs, even when faced with challenges or temptations. When we live with integrity, we build trust, respect, and genuine connections with others. Our actions inspire others to do the same, creating a ripple effect that can transform the world.

Simplifying our relationships is essential for our well-being. By fostering meaningful connections and letting go of toxic ones, we create space for healthier, more fulfilling interactions. We learn to prioritize the relationships that uplift and nourish us, while setting boundaries with those that drain our energy or undermine our self-worth.

The pursuit of purpose is a lifelong journey. It's about finding meaning and fulfillment in our work and lives, aligning our actions with our passions and values, and using our unique gifts to make a positive impact on the world. When we live a life of purpose, we experience a deep sense of satisfaction and significance that goes beyond material success or external recognition.

Resilience is the gift that allows us to bounce back from setbacks and find strength in adversity. It's about recognizing that challenges are a natural part of life, and that they can provide valuable opportunities for growth and transformation. By cultivating a positive mindset, a strong sense of self-efficacy, and a network of supportive relationships, we can navigate life's storms with grace and resilience.

The ripple effect is a reminder that our actions have consequences that extend far beyond ourselves. When we embrace simplicity, wisdom, and authenticity, we inspire others to do the same. Our choices, our words, and our actions can create a ripple effect that spreads positivity, compassion, and understanding throughout the world.

In conclusion, embracing simplicity, wisdom, and authenticity is not just a path to personal fulfillment; it's a way of life that can transform the world. By simplifying our lives, cultivating mindfulness, honoring our intuition, and living with integrity, we create a ripple effect that inspires others to do the same. We become agents of positive change, contributing to a more compassionate, just, and sustainable world.

Citation And References

This book represents the culmination of extensive research and meticulous analysis, incorporating a diverse range of sources, including numerous books, scholarly studies, and personal experiences. Additionally, I have scoured various websites to gather relevant information and data essential for the compilation of this work. I have taken every precaution to ensure the accuracy of the information presented and have diligently cited all sources to acknowledge their contributions.

Despite these efforts, the possibility of inadvertent errors remains. I deeply value the insights of my readers and appreciate any feedback that can help identify and rectify such inaccuracies. I encourage you to bring any discrepancies to my attention.

Your feedback is not only welcome but crucial, as it will aid in correcting current editions and enhancing the content of future ones. I am committed to maintaining the highest standards of accuracy and reliability in my work and thank you for your support and understanding.

Additionally, I firmly uphold the principle of freedom of speech and expression as guaranteed under Article 19(1)(a) of the Constitution of India, and I respect the diverse viewpoints and expressions of all readers.

Other Books Of The Author

1. Empowering Minds: A Journey into Women's Self-Discovery and Power
2. The Dynamics of Motivation: Catalyzing Thought into Action
3. Meditation and Mental Well Being: The Path to Inner Peace and Clarity
4. The Psychology of Child Education: Nurturing Future Generations
5. Ethical Enlightenment: A Modern Guide to Living with Integrity
6. Voices of Empowerment: Stories of Women Rising Against Odds
7. Social Psychology in Everyday Life: Understanding Human Connections
8. The Essence of Motivational Speaking: Inspiring Change in Others
9. Balancing Acts: Women, Work, and the Will to Lead
10. Guiding with Grace: Raising Children with Compassion and Awareness
11. The Power of Positive Aging: Embracing Life After Fifty
12. Building Resilient Communities: Social Work in Action
13. The Ethical Educator: Principles for Teaching and Learning
14. From Insight to Impact: Social Psychology for a Better World
15. The Ethics of Empathy: A Guide to Ethical Living
16. The Science of Empowering the Self: Navigating Life's Challenges with Psychological Wisdom
17. The Mindful Conscious Leader: Meditation Techniques for Modern Management
18. Pioneering Spirit: Women's Pathways to Leadership and Empowerment
19. Feeling to Healing: The Role of Emotional Intelligence in Child Development
20. Transformative Talks and Words of Inspiration: Insights into Motivational Oratory

21. Green Ethics: A Path to Sustainable Living
22. Spiritual Integrity: Navigating Life with Moral Compassion
23. Clean Living, Clean Society: The Ethics of Cleanliness
24. Patriotic Spirits: Building a Nation on Positive Attitudes
25. Innovative Integrity & Vibrant Visions: The Ethical and Entrepreneurial Spirit of Gujarat
26. Youthful Visions, Endless Possibilities: Inspiring Ethics and Motivation in Children
27. Living Your Legacy: How to Motivate Others by Living Your Values
28. Secret of Healing Conversations: Ethical Practices in Counselling and Therapy
29. Creative Kindness: Crafting a Life of Compassion and Creativity
30. The Power of Appreciation: How Gratitude Can Transform Your Relationships
31. Bhagavad-Gita: Messages
32. Science of Art: The New Frontier of Fashion Modernism
33. Vivekananda's Virtues: A Blueprint for Modern Living
34. Empower Her: Navigating the Path to Women's Entrepreneurship
35. The Boundless Classroom: Innovations in Global Education
36. The Language of Leadership: Communicating with Authenticity and Impact
37. The Warrior's Mantra: Deciphering the Hanuman Chalisa
38. Echoes of Empathy: Transformative Stories of Social Service
39. Artful Living: Cultivating Creativity in Your Daily Routine
40. Finding Your Why: Discovering Your Passions and Charting Your Course
41. The Role of Social Media in Shaping Self-Esteem and Interpersonal Relationships among Adolescents
42. Karma's Tapestry: Weaving a Life of Selfless Service
43. Altruistic Alchemy: Transforming Lives Through Giving
44. The Blueprint of Pro-Activeness and Productivity: Crafting Habits for Success
45. The Simplicity with Grounded Wisdom: Embracing Authenticity

in a Complex World

46. Secret of Solopreneur's Odyssey: Navigating the Path to Self-Employment
47. Exploring Tapestry of Peace: Global Perspectives on Harmony
48. The Art and Actions of Connection: Mastering Communication for Impact
49. She Governs and at the Helm: Strategies for Political Empowerment
50. Rising Above and Rising with Grace: A Woman's Roadmap to Career Mastery
51. The Effect of Networking & Connectedness: Building Strategic Alliances for Women
52. Beyond his Barriers: Women Thriving in Male-Dominated Fields
53. Secret of Inner Compass: Navigating Life with Intuition
54. Creative & Pro-Active Muses: A Celebration of Women in the Arts
55. Unburdened: The Art of Releasing the Past
56. Amplified Voices: Speeches of Women that Astonished the World
57. Secret of Manifesting Dreams: A Woman's Guide to Intentional Living
58. Ethics and Value Based Education: Reimagining Japan's School System
59. The Moral Compass Curriculum: A Holistic Approach
60. Tech with Heart: Integrating Ethics into Digital Learning
61. Honoring Virtue: Recognizing Ethical Excellence in Education
62. Raising Good Humans: A Guide to Character Development
63. The Spark Within: Nurturing Creativity in Children
64. The Teenager Whisperer: Navigating Adolescence with Grace
65. Igniting a Passion for Learning: Inspiring Lifelong Curiosity
66. The Habit Lab: Cultivating Positive Behaviors in Children
67. Seeds of Empathy: Fostering Compassion in Young Hearts
68. The Reading Revolution: Inspiring a Love of Books in Children
69. The Learning Brain: Unlocking the Secrets of Student Success
70. Teaching for All: Differentiated Instruction Strategies
71. The Time Alchemist: Mastering Time Management for Peak Performance

72. The Resilience Factor: Transforming Setbacks into Stepping Stones
73. The Healing Touch of Nature: An Introduction to Naturopathy
74. Echoes of the Past: Healing Through Past Life Regression
75. The Spiritual Healer's Handbook: Exploring Energy Medicine
76. Crystal Clarity: Unveiling the Power of Gemstones
77. The Dream Weaver's Guide: Decoding the Language of Dreams
78. Emotional Alchemy: Transforming Pain into Power
79. Sonic Serenity: Harnessing Sound for Stress Relief
80. The Entrepreneur's Playbook: Launching Your Business with Confidence
81. Productivity Unleashed: Time Management Strategies for Entrepreneurs
82. The Problem Solver's Toolkit: Creative Solutions for Business Challenges
83. The Future is Now: Emerging Trends in Business
84. The Curious Explorer: A Child's Guide to Scientific Discovery
85. Digital Pioneers: Empowering Kids in the Tech World
86. The Young Philosopher's Guide: Exploring Life's Big Questions
87. Finding Your Voice: Communication Skills for Confident Kids
88. Nature's Playground: A Child's Guide to Outdoor Adventure
89. Growing a Greener Tomorrow: A Guide to Tree Planting & Conservation
90. Driving with Purpose: Ethical Choices on the Road
91. The Healing Touch: Cultivating Compassion in Healthcare
92. Navigating the Digital Landscape: Ethics in the Age of Social Media
93. The Ethical Closet: A Guide to Sustainable Fashion
94. The Mindful Voyager: Sustainable Travel Practices
95. The Feminine Divine: Honoring the Goddesses of India
96. Sacred Sounds: Chanting Your Way to Inner Peace
97. The Yoga Path: Uniting with the Divine Within
98. Rites of Passage: Creating Meaningful Ceremonies
99. The Chakra System: A Map of Inner Transformation
100. Spiritual Sangha: Finding Community through Satsang and

Bhajan
101. Pilgrimage of the Soul: Spiritual Journeys in India

Contact

Dr. Minakshi Bansal
Social Activist
Ahmedabad, Gujarat, Bharat
minakshiindiag20@yahoo.com

|| LOKAHA SAMASTHAHA SUKHINO BHAVANTU ||

www.ingramcontent.com/pod-product-compliance
Lightning Source LLC
LaVergne TN
LVHW090318160826
845684LV00002B/19

* 9 7 9 8 8 9 4 4 6 1 9 7 7 *